Precious Memories

Blessed Hope

Other books by Tom Walton

Truly Blessed. Why Me?

Blessings Abound

RT Walton
1388 Gills Rd.
Powhatan, VA 23139
ditomwalton@verizon.net

Ordering Information:
Quantity sales. Special discounts are available on quantity purchases by corporations, associations, and others. For details, contact the publisher at the address above.
Orders by U.S. trade bookstores and wholesalers. Please contact RT Walton, Tel: (804) 492-4871
Email: ditomwalton@verizon.net

Printed in the United States of America
ISBN: 979-8-218-24167-4

It is with utmost respect that I dedicate this book to my friend and brother in Christ, Brian Kearns. Brian has been a tremendous encouragement to me on my writing journey. He, for many years, told me to share with others in verse and put those thoughts where others could be encouraged by them. Brian has also taught me by example to never quit. Though he has been in a wheelchair for over forty years he has never used that for an excuse or reason to give up. In life there will be struggles, but Brian's faith has given him victory time and time again. Thank you for your encouragement and friendship. We have many memories and also share the blessed hope of an eternity in heaven with Christ.

Cover photo by
Little Sister, Debbie

The small pond on our family farm, built in 1955, around which we had many adventures and share fond family memories from the experiences we shared there.

Psalms 19:1
The heavens declare the glory of God
and the firmament shows his handywork.

CONTENTS

A Grandmother's Tears

A grandmother is a special person, most would not deny,
So who in the world would ever make a grandmother cry?
This special person worked hard to receive this designation,
And must have had more than their fair share of agitation.

To become a grandmother one must first start out as a daughter,
And over time much will be learned that her Mom has taught her.
She must process all these things and sort the good from bad,
Then she'll become a better person from the lessons she's had.

The next chapter in the grandmother book is learned as a mother,
And most believe this chapter teaches more than any other.
There will be hard lessons learned in those mothering years,
And most Moms experience their share of frustrations and tears.

When chapter two is completed excitement begins to build,
And with joy this special lady longs for a grandmother's roll to fill.
It seems so easy when on the outside just looking in,
But by now some grandmothers have their own broken hearts to mend.

Grandmothers have all had heartaches, some no fault of their own,
Her child may have found a bad path and upon it chosen to roam.
Perhaps a grandmother now has more children for which to care,
And many tears may be shed in days and long nights of despair.

Quite often she may move more slowly than in former years,
And the hard times and new burdens may bring her to tears.
A grandmother is often placed by God to assume this important task,
Because through her many tears silent prayers were often asked.

The answers to a grandmother's prayers are her gift from above,
And because of her experiences she can convey Gods tender love.
For those who learned at the knee of their tearful grandmothers,
Those lessons may have more impact than those taught by others.

A Regular Sunday Morning

It was a regular Sunday morning, as he rubbed his sleepy eyes.
He was off from work today; no reason for him this early to rise.
Relaxing in his cozy bed he wondered what the day might bring.
Since he was off today, he had choices and could do most anything.

When his eyes came open and he saw the morning light,
He was thankful for his vision and he'd survived another night.
When he rolled over and his feet reached for the floor,
There were many options available, what to do, he wasn't sure.

In the kitchen he found his cupboard and refrigerator filled with food.
He had many choices if he was hungry and in the breakfast mood.
Through the window he could see his new car in the driveway,
And he wondered where his travels might take him today.

There was a car show at the mall, scheduled to begin at two,
With many beautiful cars on display, just looking was fun to do.
Just then, he was reminded how truly blessed he had been,
And he remembered it was Sunday, church would soon begin.

He was very thankful when he got up that he could see and walk,
And he had food and transportation and the ability to talk.
It was a regular Sunday morning; God had blessed in many ways,
And church attendance seemed the best way to offer God his praise.

It was a regular Sunday morning and the church bells were ringing.
Christians were arriving at churches and would soon be singing.
Offerings would be given and prayers for a needy brother too;
Can you think of a better thing on a regular Sunday morning to do?

A Rock For Motivation

The small sign simply stated, "a rock for motivation,"
And since I like rocks, this required a closer observation.
Rocks have fascinated me since I was a very small child,
So I stepped a little closer to the sign, and it brought a smile.

Someone had taken the time to paint words on these stones,
And the sign suggested that we could even take one home.
I've collected rocks of many colors from time to time,
But I don't have any painted stones among my many finds.

Rocks, I'm told, have existed since the universe began,
And if that's true, they must be a part of God's eternal plan.
But can a rock actually be used as a motivational tool?
If that's so, shouldn't that have been taught in school?

Many rocks are beautiful and have value that long endures,
But can they really motivated people? Of that I'm not so sure.
Some of these stones have words that may help sometimes,
But a lasting motivation would be a wonderful thing to find.

Jesus is the Rock, according to the Bible, God's Holy Word,
And His message still motivates everyone who's ever heard.
He's the Rock of salvation and on Him all can forever trust,
In fact, if you want to go to heaven, Jesus Christ is a must.

All Downhill

Runners are, perhaps a little different, compared to many.
They run because they like it, and most don't earn a penny.
I've participated in quite a few running events over the years,
But I was always careful and used only the slower gears.

Most race participants like to be familiar with the course route,
And having that knowledge can remove some runners doubt.
If the course has many steep hills they definitely do matter,
And personally I prefer a running course that's much flatter.

Many runners like to go down hills; there's less resistance,
But when the course goes up hill, it requires more persistence.
A lifetime can be much like a race; in some not-so-subtle ways,
Because we're forced to focus more on downhills as we age,

Over the hill, is a reference that all of us, by now, have heard,
Runners like it, but for old people those are discouraging words.
Downhills, we once embraced and traversed with relative ease,
But if that should be the case now; what about my aching knees?

Luke 6:34-35

And if you lend to them of whom ye hope to receive, what thank have ye? For sinners also lend to sinners, to receive as much again. But love ye your enemies, and do good, and lend, hoping for nothing again; and your reward shall be great, and ye shall be the children of the highest: for he is kind unto the unthankful, and to the evil.

Aunt Betty's Grave

We read about Aunt Betty in a letter written long ago,
And we wanted to locate her grave out of respect to show.
The letter had been penned from the large plantation house,
And was hand delivered to be mailed by the writer's spouse.

1856 was the date stamped on the letter I now hold,
But I long to hear the whole story of Aunt Betty, still untold.
Aunt Betty had made hats for the writer's daughters dear,
Which had been received by them with gladness and cheer.

I went to the cemetery located near the manor house,
And searched for Betty's marker assisted by my spouse.
We read the inscription carved on each stone with care,
But unfortunately, Aunt Betty's body wasn't resting there.

It was at that moment we realized, Aunt Betty was a slave,
And apparently was not buried near her owner's grave.
We searched diligently in the surrounding fields and woods,
But sadly, Aunt Betty had no marker in this neighborhood.

I'm sure she had been interred on some spot nearby,
But over time, graves are hard to spot with the naked eye.
Perhaps a wooden marker was carved for her with great care,
It was now gone, but Aunt Betty's story doesn't end there.

Aunt Betty had a soul which will last for eternity,
And if she received Jesus her soul had been set free.
Now you know a small part of Aunt Betty's earthly story.
We never found Aunt Betty's grave but I hope to see her in glory.

Bears Outside The Window

"There are bears outside the cabin, and they move mostly at night,"
Was what I'd been told, which brought me unimaginable fright.
We were visiting our mountain cousins who lived in a cabin made of logs,
And even now, when I see a stuffed bear, my mind is quickly jogged.

I went to bed that first night; but only at the window could I stare,
And I wondered why my Daddy had even brought us there.
I'd never seen a real bear, but that mattered not at all,
And for many years after that I didn't go outside after nightfall.

I've gotten over that experience; at least I think mostly so,
But people are sometimes fearful of things they don't know.
There are things, no doubt, that can harm us, that's for sure,
But needless worry can cripple us and be hard to endure.

Some people worry much about some catastrophic unknown,
And use every opportunity to frighten other people to the bone.
What is the solution to overcome these unfounded fears?
How can we focus better on today and be more useful to our peers?

It we believe what the Bible teaches and trust God to guide our way,
We have no need to worry; the unknown can't hurt us today.
Governments and rulers exist only by the permission of God alone,
So don't waste time worrying about some impending unknown.

No bears came in the window; I was safe in spite of my fears,
And God has kept me safe since then for all these many years.
Don't be alarmed by the predictions of a few self-exalted men.
As followers of Jesus we should be busy bringing others to Him.

Church Bingo

The excitement was building; the Bingo game had just begun,
And with only a few more numbers drawn it would soon be won.
There are some church people who enjoy a good bingo game,
But if they lose, how can a Christian say bad luck's to blamed?

I had no interest in playing in the bingo game at all,
And have a hard time getting excited when a number is called.
Without finding fault with those enjoying the game for fun,
Maybe a new version of the old game would be helpful to some.

The letters could still be called; but just leave the numbers out,
And when the game ends we could still hear the winners shout.
New games don't always catch on, and it could take some time,
But some may enjoy the new church bingo version just fine.

If "B" is called, then the players would shout "blessed,"
And possibly they could share a "blessing" with all the rest.
If, perchance, the letter "I" should by surprise then appear,
Since we're "In" church, we could tell others why we're here.

The "N" might be pulled while the excited players waited,
And since Jesus "Never" leaves us; all should be elated.
"G" of course, would pop up once in a while, no doubt,
And since "God" protects us; all could give a victory shout.

The "O" would be drawn; the odds are roughly one in five,
God is the "Only" God and in Him "Only" can we thrive.
There you have it; a brand new version of a very old game,
And if you play church bingo enough, you won't be the same.

Church People

What is it about church people that makes them distinct?
I've been one a long time so I'll share what I think.
First, they must go to church at least once in a while,
And it even helps if they're listed in the membership file.

Every institution needs members who will get involved,
And it they all take part problems can be resolved.
Unfortunately, this isn't always how things turn out,
Because too many opinions can bring disagreements about.

If an outspoken sister has a strong conviction on a matter,
Other church people may respond with hurtful chatter.
Everyone has opinions and should share when needed,
But some church people get upset when their ideas go unheeded.

Since every church person claims to be working for God,
It's amazing how often church people seem to be at odds.
Church people are more friendly when there's food on the table,
Maybe if we ate each week friendships would be more stable.

Many church people need to be much more aware,
That many people outside of church wonder why we go there.
We all need improvement and certainly we haven't arrived,
But if we don't love others our churches won't survive.

Church Seating

Everyone who's been to church knows we must sit a while,
And apparently, in our day, most would prefer to sit in style.
There was a time when every church seat was made of wood.
Wooden seats were hard but people back then all understood.

Many years later, folding contoured metal seats arrived,
And the people wondered how the old folks had survived.
Padded chairs, then came along, and were comfortable for sure,
And many questioned how grandpa's generation had endured.

These days, some still seem to focus a lot on the seating style,
And they find it hard to sit in church for even a little while.
Perhaps if we brought in recliners as another seating choice,
Some could get more information from the preacher's voice.

Recliners are much more comfortable, without a doubt,
But is comfort really what church attendance is about?
The people who came to our church when it was started,
Walked or rode a horse, but they've all now departed.

I don't think our church seating contributed to their demise.
Perhaps people then were focused more on a heavenly prize.
Has comfort become, for many, one of our worship goals?
Jesus didn't focus on comfort while redeeming our souls.

Daddy's Old Shotgun

Daddy was a bird hunter; in the south we hunted quail,
But the story I want to share isn't really a hunters tale.
It's not so much about a possession, it's more about a man,
And I hope, my point, after these few lines, you'll understand.

The old shotgun that Daddy carried isn't a fancy one,
In fact, it wasn't expensive, compared to many guns.
The name said J. C. Higgins; but I never knew that man;
Apparently, it was a part of the Sears and Roebuck brand.

J. C. Higgins, I guess, was a well known sportsman in his time,
Although famous, he couldn't beat the Daddy I called mine.
The old shotgun was a twelve gauge, of the pump style,
And each time I look at the old shotgun it brings a smile.

I don't hunt for birds with Daddy's shotgun these days,
In fact, I guess I'm more a fan of the quail, in many ways.
If per chance, I flush a covey and they quickly skyward rise,
Truth be told, I must confess, it brings a tear to my eyes.

I used to hunt birds with Daddy in the fields and woods,
And if he were here today, we'd hunt together, if we could.
But God called Daddy home to heaven many years ago,
And since I trusted Jesus, like Daddy, I plan to also go.

I cherish Daddy's old shotgun for the memories it brings,
Just because it was one of my Daddy's favorite things.
My Daddy wasn't perfect, and I never expected him to be,
But my memories are so precious because Daddy loved me.

So, if you're blessed to be a Daddy, a Father or just a Dad,
Spend time with your children, or you may wish you had.
Life is a precious gift, bestowed by our loving God above.
Spend time with your family now, and shower them with love.

Dog Foot It

My great uncle George and I often worked together on our farm.
I was a very active six years old, just attempting to do no harm.
There was a small woodworking repair job that needed to be done.
It was about eight in the morning and our work had just begun.

As he worked, I mostly watched, as he made the small repair,
But I never imagined what I could learn, just standing there.
Suddenly, without warning, uncle George smashed his left thumb,
And immediately down his arm the blood quickly began to run.

Dog foot it; he exclaimed, as his hammer fell to the floor,
Then uncle George headed to the house through the open door.
I was a little worried about his injury, it looked really bad,
But I was amazed by the fact, he didn't even seem to be mad.

About thirty minutes later he returned to the accident scene,
And shortly thereafter an important lesson for me was gleaned.
I asked Uncle George why, when he hit his thumb he hadn't cussed.
Then surprisingly, he seemed quite willing the situation to discuss.

He sadly, hung his head, and told me unfortunately he had.
To this, I quickly replied; "you didn't cuss, or even get mad."
Then he sat me down and explained a concept I didn't understand,
And his instruction has been valuable, now that I've become a man.

He told me his frustration, on the inside, mattered most,
And his heart's reaction left nothing of which he could boast.
He said the Bible tells us, if we think it, we're guilty just the same,
And even if we only say, dog foot it, of sin we must accept the blame.

Downsizing

Downsizing is a word; and well understood if you're old.
Often things accumulate if you've bought more than you've sold.
There are many extra things just lying around our house.
We must reduce possessions belonging to me and my spouse.

The old table, from a yard sale, in the corner of the den,
And some of my coin collection would be a good place to begin.
Oh yes; there are boxes of baseball cards collected years ago,
And I guess some of my cool cast iron collection could go.

Downsizing is hard; we have so many choices to be made,
But we can't keep it all; where would it ever be displayed?
What about all the things nobody would even want to buy?
I picked all of it up somewhere, but I don't remember why.

Since I'm downsizing I guess I should consider everything.
Even things about myself that to God no glory can bring.
I do sometimes have a bad attitude; I should let that go,
And I'm occasionally selfish and often let it show.

There have been times I spoke impatiently to my sweet wife;
I don't need to do that; she's loved me most of my life.
When I began to downsize, it seemed to be a daunting mission,
But now that I've started; it could put me in a better position.

Accumulated things can actually be a burden to us today,
But when possessions sprout wings we can rejoice as they fly away.
There are also inner, hidden things that can bring us down.
We have choices; so let go of everything that brings a frown.

Easter Sunday Morning

It was Easter Sunday morning; we had a busy day ahead,
No time for sleeping in today; I must get out of bed.
The Easter baskets had been filled the night before.
Our kids would love this special treat, we were sure.

We had expended much energy to get things just right,
And there was no doubt I would sleep well Sunday night.
We had even placed plastic bunny tracks in the front yard,
And to make them look authentic we worked awfully hard.

We planned to dye our own Easter eggs this afternoon,
But we must hurry, the church service would begin soon.
Our church holds an annual Easter egg hunt for our town,
And kids come from everywhere, even miles around.

When we arrived at church, the service was about to start,
And our kids, in the special Easter service, all had a part.
The program was well attended and was deemed a success,
However, on the ride home I was convicted, I must confess.

Our little Johnny simply asked why Jesus rose from the grave,
But his big sister Sally answered, "So people could be saved."
When we arrived home and the kids saw the bunny prints,
I wondered what bunny tracks had to do with Easter events.

When the kids were tucked in and our busy day had ended,
I wondered how many of my Easter efforts could be defended.
Since Easter is the time we celibate Jesus and what He did for us,
Should colored eggs, baskets and bunnies be stressed so much?

Faith For Sale

- Romans 10:17 -

There was just enough time to make, perhaps a quick stop.
We saw a yard sale setting up and we both love to shop.
It was, for me, not the most interesting sale I've found,
But one item for sale there has an impact that's profound.

It was a small wooden sign attached on both end with string,
But the only word inscribed on it can be a powerful thing.
The little wall plaque was resting beside a pile of clothes,
But I was taken back by the word the sign maker chose.

Faith, was the only word printed on a blue background,
But the message that faith conveys for me is profound.
The price said, one dollar, and was attached to the back.
I'm very thankful for the reminder on the little plaque.

I asked the people sitting in chairs behind the booth,
If what I was seeing was for sale, or had someone goofed.
They were amazed by the question asked by a stranger,
But my faith goes way back, and even includes a manger.

I then inquired, if they relied on faith on a daily basis.
They all seemed surprised, and it showed on their faces.
One lady replied that she did, and wondered why I asked,
Now the ball was in my court; teaching became my task.

I explained, the price they wanted, was way out of line,
Because you can't buy faith with money or with time.
The dear lady behind the table rose and smiled kindly at me.
Then she said. "Just take the sign, faith will set you free."

Free Tickets

There are people in this world who love the word free,
And, I must admit, on the free things list my name you'd see.
Someone had seen a small sign at the airport last week,
Advertising free tickets, so I decided to take a peek.

I went by the airport the very next day, quite excited.
They were still giving away free tickets, so I was delighted.
The fine print on the ticket, was for some, a little confusing,
But it clearly said free; so the ticket was well worth using.

The tickets were both good for one wonderful destination,
And were good forever so I got mine without hesitation.
Apparently, the purchase price for my ticket was paid long go,
And, interestingly enough, the Bible proclaims that to be so.

The free ticket which I received, was for heaven some day,
And gladly after my arrival there, forever I will always stay.
The other ticket was also to heaven at the same ticket booth,
But it wasn't at all interesting to me, to tell you the truth.

You weren't allowed to get both tickets, so all must choose,
But my choice was easy; heaven's far too important to lose.
The second ticket allowed for the holder to help pay the cost,
But if they came up short, they wouldn't go; all would be lost.

I've known a few people, whom I've met along the way,
Who were stubborn and who insisted on paying their own way.
The Bible says only Jesus could offer heaven's admission price,
Don't insist on paying for your own sins, and reject His sacrifice.

Friends

I'll admit, I'm older and some new things I don't understand,
But some more recent innovations are in very high demand.
There is apparently, a rather new way to gain more friends,
And the numbers achieved by this method seems to never end.

When I was growing up, I never thought to count each one,
The number was small, but when we gathered we all had fun.
We knew each one by name; even recognized them in a crowd,
And if one had an accomplishment we were all proud.

But with this new method one can acquire friend from all over.
I guess if you looked, you could even find one on the Mars rover.
My frustration arises from how these friendships can often end,
And many friendships don't last like they did way back when.

When differing opinions occurred between our friends,
We talked it over with the person and tried to make amends.
I understand it works differently now and seems a little mean.
Some now read they're no longer a friend on a computer screen.

It all appears so impersonal; the way things work on line,
And I think friendships meant more in those former times.
Friendships do still occur between people we actually know,
And I'm blessed to experience the love true friendships show.

It's sad how much time people spend finding friends on line.
I even found a great new friend waiting for a bus one time.
You may find a person who's desperate for a friend who cares.
Just keep your eyes and hearts open; they live most everywhere.

Fueling The Fire

The controversy had been ongoing and things were getting bad.
Some who knew about the troublesome turmoil were very sad.
It all started with differing opinions, like most disputes do,
And it was now out of hand; for men that situation isn't new.

Many with partial knowledge felt compelled to get involved,
And claimed a desire to see the situation soon resolved.
Day after day more bystanders gathered in social media land,
And some were so involved they even canceled other plans.

Of course some are never satisfied with simply listening in,
And this sadly, is a shortcoming of even well meaning men.
With momentum now gaining, the debate continued on and on.
Some offered advice at night, while others chimed in at dawn.

Social media can be entertaining even if you just listen in,
But vicarious participation is a shortcoming of far too many men.
Many repeat some online information, only recently gleaned,
And proudly interject an opinion by joining the posting scene.

There are many who would be appalled by gossip about another,
But they seem to think online chatter is different all together.
If we mind our own business and focus only on our jurisdiction,
We would be more useful to the Lord and cause less friction.

Fueling the fire was a necessary practice in my Grandpa's day,
And stirring the coals was helpful to get the fire underway.
But if Grandpa didn't need heat, he just let the fire go out.
Why can't Christians trust God more? He has a plan, no doubt.

God's Glory

Let's give God the glory and leave men completely out.
He alone deserves all the credit; can there be any doubt?
Men may have accomplishments, but only by Gods gifts.
It's only about Him, not us; I hope we don't forget.

Romans 5:1-2
Therefore being justified by faith, we have peace with God through our Lord Jesus Christ; by whom also we have access by faith into this grace where in we stand, and rejoice in hope of the glory of God.

Ephesians 1: 18-19
The eyes of your understanding being enlightened; that ye may know what is the hope of His calling, and what the riches of the glory of his inheritance in the saints.

Ephesians 2: 12-13
That at that time ye were without Christ, being aliens from the commonwealth of Israel, and strangers from the covenants of promise, having no hope, and without God in the world: But now in Christ ye who sometimes were far off and made nigh by the blood of Christ.

Grandma's Biscuits

My grandma made fresh biscuits for us almost every day.
She gave her biscuits to everyone, we never had to pay.
Hers were made by hand and crafted with great care,
And if you have a moment, her recipe I'd like to share.

First, someone had to milk the cow; a twice daily chore.
Back then cream rose to the top; unlike milk from the store.
A churn separated the cream into two parts in grandma's day;
The yellow part was butter, and the buttermilk was slightly gray.

I can't remember now everything she carefully mixed in,
But if a contest had been held, grandma's biscuits would win.
She used a homemade rolling pin to roll the dough out flat.
She could do it without looking if you stopped by to chat.

Grandma often let me eat the scraps of raw biscuit dough,
And if it was harmful for me to eat she never told me so.
The aroma of fresh cooked biscuits filled the morning air,
And when they were ready you were always in your chair.

Fresh butter and homemade jam often adorned the ones I got;
This mixture was absolutely perfect if the biscuits were still hot.
Sadly, these days, most biscuits come from the local grocery store,
And grandma's rolling pin isn't used very much anymore.

I grew up knowing grandma loved me when I was a child,
Because she often hugged me and by the way she smiled.
If you have little ones around and buy biscuits from a store,
Spend more time hugging the children and smile a little more.

Green Pastures

- Psalms 23 -

If you're not from a farm background; and today most are not,
The poem title at the top of this page may not mean a lot.
But for country people the concept is well understood,
And if your cattle have green pastures that's always good.

Green pastures are for cattle or sheep as good as it gets,
And that color is most attractive as the evening sun sets.
Cattle don't wonder very far or go astray looking for food,
Because they just eat close by if they're in the eating mood.

People, on the other hand, are fickle, even at their best,
And if another pasture seems greener they must give it a test.
Greener pastures are common when it comes to a career,
And often things look better than what we experience here.

Larger houses, land or new churches may seem better far off,
And what people have already may unfortunately be scoffed.
Things, I'm told, are always better on the other side of the fence,
And change from green to greener to some makes perfect sense.

Perhaps, a little closer inspection may be needed by some,
Because the prize we seek afar off may not be the better one.
God promised His children in Psalms chapter twenty three,
To give rest in green pastures, and that promise includes me.

God never promised greener pastures. That idea came from man.
Quite often the ideas of ambitions men may suggest a better plan.
Be thankful for the promises God gave His often wayward sheep.
God has promised green pastures where His children will sleep.

He Always Read His Bible
but he seldom spoke to men

He always read his Bible and seldom missed a day,
Because he loved to know what the Scriptures had to say.
For many years he'd been dedicated to learning more;
Bible knowledge was the most important thing, for sure.

There were many who lived near this Bible studying man,
Who knew nothing about the Bible or God's eternal plan.
They had not read the Bible and knew little about God's love,
And had no idea that Jesus was sent by a Holy God above.

Our Bible studying friend learned more week after week,
But he seldom had a conversation with people on the street.
He talked often with all the friends at church he knew,
But seemed to have no idea what else God would have him do.

Bible study, is for a Christian, required to better serve God,
But if we never share what we know, that's worse than odd.
The clear Bible mandate, given in Acts chapter one,
Is to go and spread the Gospel message of God's Son.

If we spend all our time learning only what God has to say,
We'll never be a witness to the one who needs help today.
If we shy away from people who are lost and living in sin,
Where will we find someone who's soul God would win?

He Blessed Me

God blessed me when He chose to give me life,
And those blessings continued when He gave me my wife.
I've done nothing to deserve any of the blessings that He gave,
And I certainly couldn't do anything for my soul to be saved.

I'm just a lowly sinner who has received salvation by grace,
And it's through His tender mercy that I'll someday see His face.
Each day He gives me is another blessing delivered from above,
And each step I take is a reminder of His boundless love.

The path on which He leads me was established long ago,
And as I travel through this life His compassion I must show.
The light of The Lord Jesus is sufficient to even shine through me,
And if I but follow His leading others His light may see.

I don't know when this earthly life will come to an end,
But I do know God will never leave me; on Him we can depend.
When this life is over and our pilgrimage down here is through,
I'll see my Lord in heaven and be given a body that is new.

The Bible tells of all the blessings that God desires to freely give,
And provides clear instructions on how a Christian should live.
The greatest blessing ever offered was salvation for sinful men,
But only by believing on Jesus can your blessed new life begin.

He Drove An Older Model

He always drove an older model car, as I now recall,
New cars weren't an option but it didn't matter at all.
He wore an old ball cap most everywhere he went,
But to me, this old man was surely heaven sent.

Young men need training on how to become a man,
Some advice along the way and a gentle guiding hand.
The old man spent much time with me in the fields and woods,
And many things I learned from him changed me for the good.

The old man was a good man but back then not a Christian yet,
But we worked side by side and a good example he always set.
He taught me to be honest and to look a man in the eye.
He taught me to love my family and to enjoy the evening sky.

He wore a threadbare jacket, but he said he liked it though,
And if he desired more from life, he never let it show.
The only thing my old friend lacked, as I now recall,
Was that he had not yet accepted Jesus as his Lord of all.

My old friend did come to the Lord later in his life,
To the joy of friends and family, and certainly to his dear wife.
I too rejoiced in his decision, because some good men go to hell,
And that's the reason I wanted my old friend's story to tell.

Things don't matter, new or old, it's all the same to God,
But most things we treasure pass away. Isn't that odd?
People do matter, and how we live matters too,
But only God can save a man and make all things new.

He Said God Made A Tree

The yard sale had been ongoing for a couple of hours,
And so far things were going well, with no showers.
Just then, a small framed item caught my eye,
And, in fact, I had almost walked right by.

The frame held a small poem and it looked quite old,
So I paid the fifty cent fee and to me it was sold.
I read the short poem and found it delightful,
Often, I must confess, poetry can be frightful.

At home I did some research to find more information,
And found out the poem has caused some indignation.
The critics of that day, when the piece was written,
Were certain no one, by this poem, would be smitten.

The critics took note of the simplicity of the piece.
Their objections were many and seemed not to cease.
They found it too religious to be appreciated,
But their opinion, rather soon, was much debated.

The author simply stated; "that only God can make a tree,"
And that seems obvious to ordinary people like me.
By the way, the poem became well loved by regular folks,
And soon the critics became the object of many jokes.

The small poem, called "Trees," hangs proudly on my wall,
And I don't mind God getting the credit; He deserves it all.
God did make trees; in fact, He also created man,
And I'm thankful He loves me and for my life He has a plan.

He Suffered From The Pollen

He suffered from the pollen and for him headaches were the norm,
And it was particularly acute shortly before a thunderstorm.
He loved to see the flower blooms burst forth in the spring,
And to observe this colorful display was his favorite thing.

Our sneezing friend had a dilemma he hoped to someday resolve,
Because he had a sinus problem and his plants were involved.
Life can be that way; we all quite often have ups and downs,
And when we have a problem we hope a solution can be found.

Solutions can be elusive and sometimes don't come our way,
But with the proper outlook we can still have victory every day.
To accept what we can't change and to focus on the good,
Will surely help us, and perhaps, everyone in our neighborhoods.

Romans 12: 12-14
Rejoicing in hope; patient in tribulation; continuing instant in prayer; distributing to the necessity of the saints; given to hospitality. Bless them which persecute you, bless and curse not.

Ephesians 4: 4-6
There is one body, and one spirit, even as ye are called in one hope of your calling; one Lord, one faith, one baptism, one God and Father of all, who is above all, and through all, and in all.

He Wrote A Little Poem

The poet wrote a little poem, once upon a day,
In hopes that others would like what it had to say.
Someone read the little poem and it brought to him a smile,
And since it helped him, he pondered the poem's point awhile.

Then he memorized the words of the little poem true,
And now he could recite it and bring a smile to others too.
Perhaps the little poem could help your friends today,
And they could pass it on to someone else along the way.

On and on the little poem could be passed from friend to friend,
And the words of the little poem could help many men.
No one knows, for sure, exactly what the poet had in mind,
But there is a chance a poem's words could even help mankind.

One little poem, sometimes can bring a smile to quite a few,
And perhaps that's what the poet hoped his words could do.
It's funny how a few words quickly written down,
Can sometimes be passed on and help folks for miles around.

I doubt if most poets will ever know the impact that their words,
And they certainly will never meet all the people who have heard.
After all, it's not the poet who spreads the message true,
But his hope is, that his message, might be spread by you.

Her Inscription
- Mark 14:8 -

While walking in the woods I came upon an interesting sight,
And it was particularly intriguing because it was almost first light.
On the crest of that little hill, with hardwood forest all around,
I happened upon an old cemetery; for someone sacred ground.

Apparently no one had been buried there for many years,
But no doubt, on this spot, many had shed some loving tears.
Upon further inspection I noticed one unusual resting place,
And it was the epitaph upon the stone that stopped my pace.

I stood silently as I pondered the words etched into her stone.
Apparently, the lady had called this area her earthly home.
The name on the stone was Betsy; no last name was needed,
And from the inscription all expectations for her were exceeded.

The simple quote inscribed there caused my mind to reflect,
And I wondered, what important things I had chosen to neglect.
The words placed on her stone were from a Holy Bible quote,
But the profound words seen there, for me struck a somber note.

"She hath done what she could," was for her, all that was stated,
But the implication of that statement left little to be debated.
We'll never know her lot in this life which has now ended,
But the thought conveyed by those words can only be commended.

I'm not sure what words will be inscribed on a stone someday for me,
But I'm not worthy of that kind of praise because my gifts were free.
Since God sent His only Son to pay the debt which I'd incurred,
I just want to share that message with some who haven't heard.

Hidden Talent

- Matthew 25 -

He had a hidden talent but it was obvious to few,
And most never saw his ability or what he could do.
There can be some risk with having talent not yet revealed,
And risk for some people with talent can be a scary deal.

He thought, perhaps someday, his talent would be displayed,
But time passed quickly while he waited for a better day.
Although his talent was hidden; it was his gift, no doubt,
But while it remained hidden he could never try it out.

The Bible speaks of talents; which were invested in that time.
In fact, one fearful man buried his, and didn't earn a dime.
The one who'd invested the talent with this worried man,
Took it back. To hide a talent wasn't in this investor's plan.

If we've been given a talent, or perhaps, more that one,
Those talents should be used to bring glory to God and His Son.
To leave a talent hidden, when it could be used every day,
Is far worse than never having a talent to display.

Gifts awarded to us by God should be used to bring Him glory,
And for a Christian, to hide our talent, is a very selfish story.
Use the gifts you were given to help and bless your fellowmen.
To hide the talent we've received, is in the Bible simply called sin.

Hose Water

I expect this title may seen quite odd to some,
But I bet you can relate if you ever drank from one.
Obviously things are different now in so many ways,
But I enjoyed a good drink of hose water back in my day.

It was a simple setup really and we all knew it well,
And how to beat good hose water would be hard to tell.
First you found a hose, we had several on our farm,
You might rinse before using; that wouldn't do any harm.

Screw the threads onto the spigot and run water through,
As far as I can remember that's all you had to do.
Clear, cool, refreshing water spilling forth for all to drink,
We never saw bottled water back then, I don't think.

We may have ingested a few germs and a bug or two,
But everybody drank when our ball game was through.
Our water supply came from a well in the ground,
And I think our water was the best for miles around.

Drinking from a hose did take an acquired technique,
And if some went up your nose your form may need a tweak.
Height adjustment was easy no matter your size,
Just hold the end of the hose right below your eyes.

I'll admit some bottled water today does taste divine,
But back then water was free which suited me just fine.
Now when I go to the store and see the water options there,
I am perplexed because I don't see hose water anywhere.

I Didn't Ask

I saw a stranger this morning I hadn't seen before,
I was in a hurry and brushed right by him out the door.
I Didn't ask

When reflecting on that event when I arrived at work,
My heart seemed to tell me another opportunity had been shirked.
I Didn't Ask

Who was this person anyway; why should it matter to me?
There are far too many things on my mind to speak to all I see.
I Didn't Ask

I'm burdened by the feeling deep down in my heart,
Should I have spoken before I brushed by to depart?
I Didn't Ask

Would he have replied with kindness and encouraged me today?
I guess I will never know since I ignored him on my way.
I Didn't Ask

Could he have had a small request; a need I could have met,
Or did he have a heavy burden that hinders him yet?
I Didn't Ask

Does he know the Savior who died to set all sinners free;
Was I the one God was leading to share; was it me?
I Didn't Ask

I Told My Puppy

The meeting had been long and some tempers had flared.
Some said things in public that should not be shared.
I was frustrated by all the back and forth I'd heard.
In fact I was angry; the unkind outbursts were absurd.

I told my puppy what happened when I got back to my house.
She sat there patiently, with little reaction, as quiet as a mouse.
She didn't seem at all upset as I gave her the details,
And from time to time she patiently wagged her puppy tail.

It had been quite stressful for me and I told her so,
But if my puppy was upset, it certainly didn't show.
When I finally finished talking and calmed down a bit,
My puppy came over beside me where she often sits.

When I reached over and gently patted her on the head,
She seemed not to have been affected by anything I said.
Puppies don't get upset by things beyond their control,
And perhaps puppy owners shouldn't either, if truth be told.

Colossians 1:27
To whom God would make known what is the riches
of the glory of this mystery among the gentiles; which
is Christ in you the hope of glory.

I'm a Grownup

Everyone said it would eventually come to pass,
And it did happen, perhaps just a little too fast.
I'm a grownup now; how we all wanted to be one someday,
And we all looked forward to it as children while at play.

It has turned out a little different than most first thought,
All grownups notice each time something must be bought.
Grownups do get to drive the car; not sit in the back seat,
And the better view up front has been hard to beat.

Unfortunately, if the car breaks down while we're on our way,
It's has become my responsibility, for the repair I must pay.
Taxes, insurance and tuition each become the grownup's lot,
And the bills still seem to pile up if we're ready or not.

Yes, I'm a grownup, no longer growing up but out,
And some may by now even suffer from painful gout.
Glasses or hearing aids are often needed to safely arrive,
Another problem for older grownups who still can drive.

We visit the doctor now with a large array of aches and pains,
But if our investments have done well we have more earthly gain.
If we had the option of going back to our childhood youthful roll,
Would we give up the grownup privileges earned by growing old?

I'm Just a Puppy

I'm just a puppy, not even close to being a big dog,
And I spend most of my day just sleeping like a log.
When I do wake up, adventure is often on my mind,
And a more active companion may be hard to find.

I am quite curious and will explore everything in sight,
And to keep me out of trouble may take all your might.
I am a very good puppy; I don't think a bad one exists,
But to a puppy every temptation can be hard to resist.

Meal time is an adventure; even most people would agree,
And it's important to step aside when food's in front of me.
I'm certainly not a picky eater like some small children are,
But I've been known to lose my meal while riding in the car.

Bathroom training is a challenge and can be hit or miss,
But please be patient, I hope to soon master even this.
I do occasionally chew a few things here and there,
And I hope my latest victim wasn't your antique chair.

Bed time is a wonderful time for a furry friend like me,
I love to snuggle and fit quite nicely right behind your knee.
Sometimes I can be a little restless and move around a bit,
But I promise to work harder while you train me to sit.

I'm just a puppy and so glad I came to live with you,
I'll do my best not to bark too much like some puppies do.
If you can be patient with me and give me time to grow,
I promise to be your faithful friend wherever we may go.

In A Hurry

He was always in such a hurry; so many places to go,
With never time to reflect as he scurried to and fro.
He must check on this or that with no time to reflect,
And he never took a day off or took time just to rest.

All roosters are like that wherever you may roam,
As they stay busy always around their barnyard homes.
Roosters don't have large brains, as research seems to show,
And they can't evaluate options while quickly on the go.

Men, on the other hand, have large brains and the ability to choose,
Options that are best for them and can consider other views.
So why not slow down a bit? Perhaps shift into a slower gear,
And make a difference around you since that's why you're here.

1 Thessalonians 1:3
Remembering without ceasing your work of faith, and labor of love, and patience of hope in our Lord Jesus Christ, in the sight of God and our Father.

It Said
The Obituary

It said many nice things that this person had done,
And it seemed like her life had been an active one.
She had been a kind person and befriended most she knew,
So this report was positive when her life was through.

She was quite outgoing and served her church very well,
And attended many church functions the obituary tells.
Being an active person she loved the great outdoors,
And of her love for hiking all her friends were quite sure.

Sports were important to her according to all she knew,
And a good game brought her joy through and through.
She loved her pets dearly and gave them the very best care,
And while taking them on a walk they enjoyed her being there.

There is one thing not mentioned in her obituary review,
And I hope it took place before her life down here was through.
Nothing was mentioned about her standing before the Lord,
And when life was finished was He the one she most adored?

She wasn't the only one eulogized in the paper today,
In fact, we will all someday in the paper pass this way.
The Bible teaches that belief in Christ is heaven's only gate,
So trust in Him today my friend before it's eternally too late.

It's a Weed

It started as a simple discussion between my wife and I,
And soon became a disagreement, let me tell you why.
A very unusual plant had emerged from the ground,
The likes of which neither of us had ever found.

I told her it was a weed, there was no doubt in my mind,
And suggested we pull it until a replacement we could find.
However, she was insistent and thought a flower it might be,
So with some reluctance I relented. In time we would see.

Many days passed as our mystery plant continued to grow,
And I was sure someday the truth of my hunch would show.
She, on the other hand, seemed quite content to watch and wait,
And revealed no hint of worry regarding our new plant's fate.

One night our puppy indicated it was time for bathroom relief,
And what I saw when I went outside I viewed with disbelief.
Our new plant, my weed, her flower, had revealed its identity,
And its blossoms showed forth golden splendor for all to see.

We stood in amazement at the magnificence of the display,
Which revealed its beauty in darkness, but in daylight went away.
Her flower, or my weed, it makes no difference anymore.
The blossoms provide a blessing no viewer can ignore.

It's Not Easy Being Me

"It's not easy being me;" said the bullfrog to the toad,
As they discussed their problems near bullfrog's watery abode.
"What makes your life so hard?" Said the toad covered with warts;
You don't have it all that bad, according to the recent reports.

The toad further stated that he had many problems too.
Hopping around on dusty roads wasn't an easy thing to do.
Bullfrog had an idea; since frowns now covered both faces.
"How about we, for one night, exchange living spaces?"

They agreed to meet again tomorrow, near the small pond's shore,
And with new information to continue their discussion a little more.
Bullfrog couldn't sleep at all well with no watery surroundings,
And toad couldn't swim well and found this limitation astounding.

They met again by the pond shore as planned early the next day,
And it was surprising just what each amphibian friend had to say.
Bullfrog stated that he'd been wrong and apologized to the toad,
And toad asked for forgiveness for complaining about the dusty road.

The moral of this little story should be clear for humans too,
Complaining about our circumstances, is for people, nothing new.
Perhaps a more positive outlook and a more thankful heart,
Would make a huge difference for each new day we start.

Judas Heard The Sermons

but he missed the truth

- Matthew 26 -

He walked beside Jesus for almost three full years,
Where he saw people healed, as Jesus took away many tears.
He heard the Lord's sermons that were preached to men,
And he knew what Jesus taught about unforgiven sin.

He saw the five thousand fed and watched the lame man walk,
But he somehow was satisfied just to simply, talk the talk.
He found a way to make money by betraying the Lord;
Money now in his pocket, with the pharisees he got on board.

Judas very soon met an untimely end; the Bible record shows,
But the teaching of Jesus didn't recommend the path he chose.
Judas sealed his own fate by rejecting what Christ had to say,
And everyone we meet must someday decide in a similar way.

If we read the Lord's words recorded in scripture and believe,
Then we'll make the best choice and Salvation we shall receive.
But if we reject God's instruction and seek some better way,
We, like Judas, will parish and inherit only eternal dismay.

Some may hear good preaching and know what they must do,
But like Judas, some miss the message, when the sermon's through.
Jesus is, "the Way, the Truth and the Life," sent by our Holy God.
Don't miss His message and choose only a religious facade.

Just A Box Of Pictures

Our auction sale was scheduled to start promptly at nine,
So we were busy sorting boxes to be placed in lines.
The crowd had gathered and was anxiously milling around.
Perhaps some hidden treasure in a box today might be found.

Some boxes were filled with glass and required great care,
But there were also lighter ones scattered here and there.
Our job was to check each box and make the contents known;
Anything from antique door nobs to very old telephones.

One small box seemed to stir the interest of quite a few,
So we made sure we kept it away from the morning dew.
It contained some family photos taken many years ago,
But why they caused so much interest, we didn't know.

Some had known the subjects and wanted a closer look,
And though the sale had started spent all the time it took.
A dear lady looked at one picture with a knowing smile,
And acknowledged, to others, she hadn't seen it in a while.

Many of the loved ones depicted were no longer here,
And just seeing them again, brought to some, a thoughtful tear.
It's interesting how many times families seem to drift apart,
But sadly, much later, many may have a change of heart.

Even large families will eventually be seen only in pictures,
But there can be another gathering according to the scriptures.
All who trust in Jesus will assemble in the sweet by and by,
Where no tears will ever be shed near those mansions on high.

Just A Small Church

He had attended a small church with very few members,
And they didn't have many activities to be remembered.
Church people stay busy; there are many things to be done,
And activities take a lot of effort, with help from everyone.

Big churches must find it easy; they have a large worker pool.
They have many people well qualified to teach Sunday school.
Small churches often have far less people to go around,
And enough people to do everything may never be found.

Unfortunately, even large churches can have staffing gaps,
Could it be the people there become complacent; perhaps?
In a small church everyone knows that workers are needed,
And the work of the Lord must keep going on unimpeded.

Some may leave the small busy church to attend a larger one,
Where some don't work very hard and people have more fun.
Many churches like the big crowds which activities often bring,
But are large activities the most important Christian thing?

The Bible does have some instruction about activity rules,
And almost all think it best to have a good Sunday School.
But what about large group trips, maybe to the Holy lands,
Or the day trips to hear a highly acclaimed concert band?

Frankly, our small church can't do all those fancy things,
In fact, some may cringe when our small church choir sings.
The Bible simply mandates that we make a joyful noise,
So I wonder what planning guide some big churches employ.

Every local church exists only to advance the cause of Christ,
Although many large extravagant activities may be nice.
Perhaps a consistent focus on Jesus and what He came to do,
Would benefit us all and the people outside of church too.

Just An Old Barn

It was just an old barn standing in the quiet woods,
But God used the structure greatly in our neighborhood.
Some men had an idea, they thought sent from above,
It involved the old barn and the message of God's love.

The barn became a meeting place for those faithful few,
Who sought God's direction for what He would do.
A small church was erected by them upon that clayey sod,
And all were convinced it was only by the grace of God.

A cemetery was started nearby for those who passed away,
Awaiting the sure hope and promise of resurrection day.
Jesus had satisfied the debt each owed because of sin,
And all will go to heaven if their faith and trust was in Him.

The old barn is gone now, as are the early faithful few,
But what God is doing here may be far from through.
Generations have come and gone; many names and faces,
But the Gospel is still going forth from this and many places.

It's not about the old barn or the church now in its place,
But it is, and always will be, about God and his love and grace.
Buildings, pastors, teachers and members, more that just a few,
But until the Lord calls us home our work down here isn't through.

God has always existed; but for barns and buildings that's not so.
God will fully equip his faithful servants wherever they may go.
Jesus promised to prepare a place for us in heaven far above,
And all who go there someday owe it all to the Saviors abiding love.

Listening

Once upon a time there was a very loud little bunny,
And he often told jokes, which he thought were funny.
His mother had warned him to be quiet and listen more,
Because there were dangers around; of that she was sure.

Unfortunately, our little cotton-tailed furry bunny friend,
Didn't take her timely advice and met an untimely end.
Before you get upset; this little bunny is make believe,
But there is a listening principle that men should receive.

Often people just want a compassionate listening ear,
And they only need a friend who's willing to hear.
Many times a hurting person doesn't desire our advice,
And to have someone to listed would be awfully nice.

There are some these days, who only listen to speak,
Because a chance to give their advice is all they seek.
As these, would be hearers, formulate their next reply,
The one who wants a listener if left to sadly wonder why.

Humans, like bunnies, have two ears but mouths, only one,
And some choose to talk from morning till the day is done.
Mamma rabbit had good advice for her talkative offspring,
And if he'd listened more, perhaps today he could sing.

There is a time for advice, and many who need it will ask,
But just because someone speaks; talking's not our task.
Perhaps a friend just wants to share a burden of their heart;
They may not need a speaker; just play the listener's part.

Looking Down

Looking down may seem an unusual poem theme,
But with a little explanation I hope you'll see what I mean.
Growing up on our farm I looked down quite a lot,
And I found many arrowheads on my secret spot.

While looking for these ancient artifacts from the past,
One must focus on the ground and not move very fast.
Of course, looking down was needed so you wouldn't trip,
But even when careful one could fall and cut your lip.

I never looked down much after dark when the stars were out,
Because looking up at them was fascinating without a doubt.
So many stars to look at and they appeared every night,
And to watch them twinkle was for me a wonderful delight.

As I navigate this one and only life on earth I'll ever get,
I can't help noticing the gazing direction of some I've met.
For me looking upward reflects a more optimistic view,
While looking downward seems to sadden quite a few.

Down and out, down trodden, you sure look down today,
Perhaps, looking up is the more joyful and better way.
I've read in the Bible about a wonderful place called Glory,
But an eternity in heaven isn't the only relevant story.

Jesus came to earth with a message of eternal hope for man,
And those who believe on Him need no other long term plan.
Today is the best day to look up and in victory begin to live,
No time to loose looking down, we have uplifting gifts to give.

Love Thy Neighbor
no exceptions

We were off for a day trip; and it was a beautiful day,
The sun was shining, winds were light; fall foliage on display.
When we reached our destination at about half past ten.
It was time to visit a small museum owned by our friend.

As we exited the car, I noticed a sign in the museum yard;
The implication of the stated concept, for some, may be hard.
Love thy neighbor, were the words boldly printed on the sign,
But the words printed underneath, touched this heart of mine.

"No exceptions." Just a simple statement, understood by all;
But the application of that concept can cause some to be appalled.
The Bible tells us to love our neighbor; we must obey that command,
But many men may take exception to this further implied demand.

Just who is my neighbor? That could get some off the hook.
But the application of the last phraise requires a closer look.
Our neighbor may live close or they may live much farther away,
But isn't each one I meet, actually my neighbor today?

I asked my friend if I could acquire a copy of his sign,
Because I needed to see it often to soften this hard heart of mine.
As I look out of my front window, my new sign is on display.
My hope is, it will be seen and read by all who pass this way.

Our day trip has now ended and the new sign stands in our yard.
No doubt, some who read it, may find the concept very hard.
We may not agree with the choices all men make who pass this way,
But God has given us the grace to honor what the sign has to say.

Making Memories

Materials are normally needed if something is to be made,
And the lack of them could cause the project to be delayed.
To make a sturdy picnic table a few materials are needed,
And without them the picnic outing would be impeded.

To make a birthday cake we most often need eggs and flour,
And without those ingredients the party would certainly sour.
While pondering a maker's dilemma with deficient supplies,
I came to a conclusion which most people would not deny.

Memories, I've concluded, often take only a few resources,
Since most of my memories involved only time and choices.
My Mom and Dad each found time for me along the way,
And I still remember how that made me feel while at play.

I guess perhaps, to make a memory, more could be required,
But just a little time from others fulfilled my childhood desires.
We all have memories; that's an important part of living life,
And some of those can involve occasional conflict or strife.

Today, in addition to time, I think more effort would be good,
To encourage other people who now live in our neighborhood.
Get involved in the lives of others and donate a little time,
And plant a fond memory in your lonely neighbor's mind.

Margie's Way

There's a small sign on a driveway near where I live.
Placed there as a tribute to a Christian lady who loved to give.
"Margie's Way" the sign simply states, posted by the road,
And it marks the driveway to Margie's former humble abode.

I was blessed to serve with Margie, teaching the church youth,
But it was her life that revealed her testimony was the truth.
She lived a simple life, with few earthly riches to be claimed,
But each time you saw her, she was always the same.

Margie was quiet and shy; often with a subtle little grin,
And the children were anxious for time with her to begin.
She went to the doctor; something didn't feel just right,
And the doctor revealed to her that cancer was her plight.

All her friends offered prayer for this dear lady in need.
Healing, with full recovery, they prayed she might receive.
The prognosis for her got worse; hers was a serious case,
But doctor's words couldn't change this lady, filled with grace.

Our pastor went to the hospital to share an encouraging word,
But her reply to his statement was the wisest I've ever heard.
The pastor said he was sure that Margie would be OK,
Then calmly, she simply stated, she'd be fine either way.

Margie had trusted Jesus; He was her Lord and guide,
So, no matter the outcome, in His grace she would abide.
If you should pass her old driveway, marked with the little sign,
Take a moment to thank Jesus; Margie's in heaven, doing fine.

My Credentials

I'm honored to have been invited to speak to you today my friend,
And I thought it appropriate to share the credentials on which I depend.
My pedigree is quite plain compared to most speakers out there,
But I'm thankful you came out to hear what I have to share.

I was a normal country kid raised on a small family farm,
And I'm thankful for my rural roots and natures simple charms.
I did manage to finish high school, which surprised quite a few,
And even went to college before my formal education was through.

As to what I have to offer; and my hope is you will be blessed,
I think it fitting that my lack of credentials should be stressed.
I'm just a poor sinner saved by a Holy loving God's grace,
And I'm thankful for His only Son who on a cross took my place.

The Bible tells us that all our righteousness is but filthy rags,
So obviously no mere mortal has anything on which to brag.
I came into this world equipped with a small but sinful heart,
So from the beginning I had no worthy information to impart.

I'm just a poor beggar showing others where to find bread too,
That's what I want to tell others before my days are through.
With my credentials covered; no more introduction needed,
A loving God, His only Son, and His Word to be heeded.

My New Used Driver

I'm an old golfer, at least most would think so.
No doubting the old part, but golfing I still often go.
I seen to struggle quite a bit, mostly from tee to green,
And I may be the least talented golfer some have ever seen.

I purchased a new driver for $2.65 at our local thrift store,
And I was hoping it would help my game, but I wasn't sure.
It's a beautifully crafted club, none would dare dispute,
And I was hopeful it would lower the score I often shoot.

I know practice may be needed to overcome a hook or slice,
But any observer must admit my new club does look nice.
Unfortunately my new driver may have a few drawbacks,
And this becomes more obvious when a golfer's talent lacks.

Recently I took my new used driver out to the local links.
I realized senior golfers might need to work out a few kinks.
A few adjustments were needed to help this old golfer's game,
But if they don't work my new used driver's not to blame.

It was a perfect day to try out my lightweight new shaft,
But on hole one I drove my ball over hole three's cart path.
When I finally located my ball behind a large pine tree,
I was thankful I play alone so no other golfer could see,

Well, I don't ever plan to give up; old golfers seldom do,
But my brand new used driver now resides in storage unit two.
I'm sure this won't be the last sad golfing story ever told,
Because a new clubs may not help much when you get old.

My Older Sister

What is it about an older sister that brings us to attention?
They can often be a little bossy, I think it fair to mention.
I had an older sister, born two years before my arrival,
And I think she felt some pressure to assure my survival.

She was so very serious, but her little brother; not so much.
He wasn't at all concerned with small details and such.
I already had a mother, so there was no need to have another,
But my sister wanted me to stand up straight while together.

I loved to play outside and of those activities I never tired,
But my older sister stayed inside, which I seldom desired.
I thought she was very smart; her grades were always high,
But mine were sometimes low and I didn't really care why.

Often when we went somewhere she wore a pretty dress,
But according to the family photos I was usually a mess.
She occupied much of her time just reading heavy books,
While I stayed busy exploring our farm's creeks and brooks.

Events can take place that cause us to adjust our attitude,
And sadly, we may run out of time to express our gratitude.
My sister got sick at forty years old, and sadly passed away.
I must tell you, I now regret, how I spent some early days.

Siblings don't always see eye to eye; of course that's true,
But if you would take some advice; here's some for you.
Love you family members and gives hugs while you can,
And I promise you won't regret it; hugs are the better plan.

A note from my older sister in a book she gave me fifteen months before she died. "To my dear brother with love at Christmas and all our lives."

Your sister,
Sandra
12/25/85

No Fruit Inspectors Needed

Church signs can be interesting, and I've see my fair share.
Often the church name is listed and the pastor there.
Sometimes you could see a catchy phrase on a sign,
But I heard of one recently that you won't often find.

"No Fruit Inspectors Needed Here;" was written after the name,
And I thought that could be a little hard for a pastor to explain.
Fruit inspectors are employed normally for just one task.
And if fruit quality is in question, inspectors must be asked.

But why would a church ever have need for fruit inspectors?
Wouldn't they be needed more in the citrus growing sectors?
I heard one Christian say, to judge another, they never would.
God alone is qualified to judge in this and every neighborhood.

But unfortunately there are some who like to inspect other's fruit,
But that's not judging; of this they seem completely resolute.
God calls Christians to bare fruit and to impact the lives of others.
Sometimes we do that alone, but often we work together.

A church fruit inspector is another name for a judge of men,
And if you look closely, in the Bible, God calls that a sin.
There's no time for a Christian to inspect the work of others.
Our effort should be used for harvesting fruit for God together.

Old Folks

Old folks have been around since shortly after the creation of man,
And to receive this designation many years their lives must span.
Ups and downs have been experienced by them many times,
And each one has stories from when they were in their prime.

Old folks have earned their fair share of aches and pains,
And we understand if they occasionally may complain.
When I was little there were three old folks in our home,
And I saw them often while on my adventures I roamed.

Each shared past experiences from their long ago youth.
I found their stories interesting and I knew each told the truth.
None of the three ever owned a phone or even drove a car,
They never flew in an airplane, or even once traveled very far.

They were all from the country and worked hard on our farm.
They never got in trouble or did other people any harm.
Each lived a simple life and have long ago passed away,
But I still remember their stories and what each had to say.

If you have children who don't have any old folks around,
Let them meet some older people; they can easily be found.
Now we call old folks, senior citizens; sounds better I guess today,
But children can learn much from what the old folks have to say.

One More Time

We were assembled this morning to offer God our praise,
Because He has blessed us all in so many ways.
Just then, an older black brother rose to his feet,
What would the old man say, now standing by his seat?

The words he chose were simple, and his voice was loud and clear.
He then boldly praised God for, one more time, bringing him here.
The brother was very old, and no doubt had attended many times,
But the words he chose still echo in this busy heart of mine.

One more time to gather on this side of glory.
One more time to hear the loving Savior's story.
One more time to hear the children sing praises to the Lord.
One more time to assemble with sisters and brothers of one accord.

One more time to worship our Holy God in this place.
One more time to step away from life's hectic pace.
One more time to bow my head and petition for a brother.
One more time to encourage an expectant mother.

One more time to place my meager offering in the plate.
One more time to confess my sin; next week may be too late.
This Sunday could be the last Sunday we have to pass this way,
So with all my heart I come this morning to praise Jesus for today.

Outdoor Recreation

It's interesting how definitions can over time often change,
And if you've been around awhile you may think that's strange.
Outdoor recreation is considered a major industry these days,
But we never thought about our activities in those ways.

I never saw a golf course or an outdoor recreation place,
But we did spend a lot of time in open outdoor space.
I spent many hours at a brook we called Stigger's branch,
In fact, I played there every time I had the chance.

There were minnows swimming there every time I went,
And I enjoyed it so much, it was at least a weekly event.
We also often recreated in the nearby fields and woods,
And the local kids played outside together when we could.

All the nearby farm ponds had fish free for anyone to take,
I preferred mine fried but some enjoyed a good fish baked.
There were toad frogs hiding under almost every large stone,
And I spent much time looking for them; no time for a phone.

We also participated in outdoor activities called chores,
And most of mine, I'm glad to say, were done outdoors.
We fed the chickens, milked the cows and slopped the hogs,
And if time was left we looked for lizards under rotten logs.

I think I should mention all these activities were free,
And every hill or dip on our farm had potential activity.
Outdoor recreation wasn't big business, way back then,
But we had fun and the chance of finding trouble was slim.

Puppy Training

Nothing worth having comes easily, or so I've been told.
My efforts began in earnest when I was just eight weeks old.
My new family seemed nice when I left my mother's side,
And for the first few nights it was hard and I often cried.

Soon I realized my life's mission had suddenly changed,
But it might not be easy to get my new family trained.
I figured out that patience would be needed for this task,
If I expected my owner to respond each time I asked.

At first it was a power struggle, I must freely admit,
But I eventually taught my owner how to entice me to sit.
I just remained patient until she offered me a treat,
Now I sit down when I'm hungry and want a snack to eat.

My new family needed exercise like all humans do,
So I whine to go outside so they'll take a walk too.
Now we walk together often and hardly miss a day,
I just pull them with my leash when it's time to play.

I take my Mom to the dog park for a change of venue,
So she can see what other puppy parents have learned to do.
It was there I trained my new Mom to throw a ball to me,
But she can't catch it in her mouth; how hard can that be?

Sandbox Lessons

We played in a homemade sandbox when I was small,
The sides were made from wood and about ten inches tall.
Each corner had a small seat, but we didn't sit very long,
And from time to time we sang children's songs.

We learned to share in the box because toys were few;
An important lesson because sharing we all must do.
Daddy built our sandbox and placed it in the side yard,
His actions taught us we were loved even if times were hard.

Often my two sisters gladly shared the sandbox with me.
We spent many hours in the shade of that old maple tree.
The sand to fill the box came from the creek on our farm;
There was lots of sand there so taking some did no harm.

We had cats who roamed freely and shared out territory.
We learned to remove lumps of sand; that's another story.
When other kids came to visit they played in the box too;
We learned to play together; that's what neighbors do.

We learned when our Mom called we should not delay,
And if we followed her instructions we had a better day.
Perhaps children these days, while playing on their phones,
May miss some lessons we learned near our country home.

Selling Jesus

The old picture of Jesus hung for many years on a rusty nail,
Then someone suggested we put the relic in our church yard sale.
It was very old and had experienced much wear and tear,
And when the suggestion came up, no one seemed to care.

Our sale started last Saturday morning promptly at eight,
And shoppers know the best things go early, so don't be late.
Shortly after our annual church yard sale got under way,
We noticed the Lord had provided for us a beautiful day.

As we welcomed eager shoppers to our fundraising event,
I had no idea the message we may have inadvertently sent.
When an elderly lady approached the table that I manned,
I had no idea what she thought or the question she planned.

Are you selling the picture of Jesus at your table today?
I don't think that's a good idea, she went on to say.
Frankly, I hadn't thought about what that sale might imply,
Although I fully understood the sacrifice given when He died.

Jesus was sold for thirty pieces of silver once in the past,
But the sacrifice He gave was free and will forever last.
No; we can't sell Jesus, He was a gift from God above,
And without receiving that gift we will never know true love.

The picture of Jesus is hanging again in its familiar place,
And we know it's only an artist's rendition of our Savior's face.
The picture is old, none can argue that. Who would even try?
But if you ask why we worship here; Jesus is the reason why.

Serving God

God called me to be a servant, I know that's true,
But just exactly what would He have me to do?

God doesn't need me to send Him a home cooked meal,
But if I cook for my lonely neighbor, how would God feel?

God might have leaves that need raking, but I don't think so,
However, I could rake some for an older friend I know.

God doesn't go to the doctor so He doesn't need a ride,
But is their someone that might need me today by their side?

I don't think God needs me to read for Him a story,
But if I read to a small child could that bring God glory?

If God asked me to cut for Him a load of firewood,
He might have me deliver it to someone in my neighborhood.

God doesn't need me to send Him a birthday card,
But maybe I should reach out to one for whom times are hard.

Serving God is not always easy, but is best done with a smile.
If God doesn't need something today, just serve others for a while.

1 Peter 1:3
Blessed be the God and Father of our Lord Jesus Christ, which according to his abundant mercy hath begotten us again unto a lively hope by the resurrection of Jesus Christ from the dead.

Set A Goal This Morning

Goal setting has often been used for a motivational tool,
And I remember my coaches used this technique in school.
They seemed to have goal setting down to a science,
And even had many ways to insure our compliance.

With team sports, these days, mostly off of my plate,
I wonder should I still be setting goals, or is it too late?
I'm very thankful that I'm still able to move around,
And I'm sure someone with needs could still be found.

That can be my first goal; find someone to help each day,
Surely we can locate one who needs my help in some way.
I feel better already, with just one goal fixed on my mind,
So I need to start my search among the local mankind.

My coaches posted several goals on the locker room door,
So an additional goal, set by me, could help even more.
With my long past school days now fresh on my mind,
Perhaps, I could learn a lesson from the needy one I find.

Today I must find someone who needs a helping hand,
And then see what can be learned from them; that's my plan.
Goal setting is still important and can bring long term success,
But caring about other people is a goal that God will bless.

She Had A Question

Are you blessed?

She worked at a produce market in Seattle called Pike's place.
When I noticed her, she had a distant expression on her face.
She had seen the mask I wore on this crowed market day,
And I was caught by surprise by what the lady had to say.

"Are you?" Were the only words she suddenly spoke out loud,
Though I could hardly hear her words over the noisy crowd.
Just then, I suddenly realized she had read the mask I wore,
And I thought she had spoken to me, but I wasn't really sure.

My mask simply said, "Blessed." Which is for me true,
And I thought more about that when my day was through.
I then quickly told the young lady, that I was blessed indeed,
But the look she gave portrayed someone with many needs.

I then boldly asked, in my reply, if she found herself blessed,
But her remorse filled rebuttal shook me, I must confess.
She stated that she was not; and in fact, she was cursed,
And after work she had plans to visit her voodoo doctor first.

She turned and slowly walked away, without another word.
I could only stand speechless, haunted by what I'd heard.
God had blessed me, time and time again, without fail,
And I feel compelled to tell you this heartbreaking tale.

This lady lived in Seattle and worked in the market there,
But surely there are other lost people most everywhere.
If we are indeed blessed by the only true God above,
Shouldn't we be eager to share the message of His love?

Speculation

What is it about speculation that intrigues us so much?
We often hear of some feared problem while keeping in touch.
Even those dear people who claim never to speculate,
May worry, and be fearful, if they arrive somewhere late.

Some are quite involved in politics and back a candidate,
Who will be elected by a landslide they confidently speculate.
But when the big election has ended and all votes have been cast,
They wonder why they made a their decision on him quite so fast.

Men sometimes speculate in romance to pick a mate for life,
But alas; some who look nice may not make a good wife.
Women, on the other hand, while seeking a future man,
May find with more information it's best to carefully plan.

Some often speculate on the success of a favorite team,
And many people out there know exactly what I mean.
But when the season has ended and all scores are in the book,
Perhaps their optimism could have used a closer look.

The prodigal son of the Bible, speculated on a better life,
But his experiment was unsuccessful and he found only strife,
His father though, still loved him and welcomed the son's return,
So perhaps speculators may have some lessons to be learned.

Speculation can be tricky and often doesn't turn out well,
But the Bible only deals with truth, with the future it foretells.
Trust God and His Word and believe on His only Son,
Speculation is risky; only by Jesus can a soul be won.

Surrounded By Sinners

Another hard day of troubles and fears grip my soul,
Because if you're surrounded by sinners it takes a toll.
When I leave the comforts of my home and go to my job,
I feel like sometimes I'm surrounded by the mob.

There are homeless people often sleeping beside the street,
And I certainly wouldn't speak to some of the dirty people I meet.
Sinners, sinners everywhere as far as the human eye can see,
But I'm very thankful I trusted Jesus from sin to set me free.

The highlight of my week arrives on Sunday mornings,
But sometimes the preacher offers some somber warnings.
Often he speaks of prideful men controlled by sinful hearts,
And we seem to have many like that around these parts.

Suddenly I understood the message loud and clear.
I was surrounded by mostly redeemed sinners here.
Apparently there are only two types of people in any place,
Sinners without Jesus and those who have received His Grace.

The sinners I avoided last week with judgment on my face,
Seem somehow different now, because I was once in their place.
Where would I be if someone had not told me of God's love,
And shared the Gospel message of salvation from above?

This new revelation led me to a very important fact,
Something I had forgotten and some insight I seemed to lack.
All who will enter heaven's gates are sinners saved by grace.
So, perhaps I should spread the Word before I leave this place.

The Average Christian

Is there anything about average that gets our attention?
Are average accomplishments really worthy of mention?
I guess when we start out, average could be a goal,
But most don't brag about average things, truth be told.

The average baseball team wins half of their games,
And for a football team the numbers are about the same.
The average golfer doesn't ever make it to the tour,
And troubles incurred while golfing can be hard to endure.

How about the average neighbor living down the street,
Do you think of them fondly when at the store you meet?
When a situation arises that needs to be addressed,
Does the average neighbor chip in and do their best?

When we send our children off each day to school,
Do we hope they have an average teacher as a rule?
When the honor roll is posted for all to behold,
Are we excited about the straight "C" honor roll?

How about the average Christian in the congregation,
What is required to receive the average designation?
Attendance will be average for most on this list,
And participation on work day will be hit or miss.

When the offering plate is passed down his pew,
He gives just like most average church members do.
Jesus came to earth to save sinners, just like you and me,
But it wasn't an average price He paid to set us free.

The Beauty Contest

The announcements were posted all over town,
And surely contestants would come from all around.
Since beauty is appreciated by everyone we know,
We hold a beauty pageant every two years or so.

The ladies were all excited to find out who might win,
But waiting was hard until the event could begin.
Of course, it does matter what each judge desires,
So after they're selected, perhaps we should inquire.

The big day finally arrived and with ten finalists selected,
Each made much preparation; no details were neglected.
All did their very best; that could never be debated,
And everyone in town, for the winner, would be elated.

When the judges had conferred and the results were in,
All in the crowd were excited to see who would win.
When the final results were announced and read aloud,
There was amazement experienced by all in the crowd.

The judging was now complete and the tally made known,
But all were confused by results read into the microphone.
Each contestant had received exactly the same scores,
So every participant had won as they exited the doors.

Upon further questioning on how the scores were tabulated,
Each concluded all the contestants were by God created.
God makes no mistakes and all are beautiful in His sight,
So they decided each contestant's beauty was exactly right.

The Blind Hog And The Acorn

"Even a blind hog finds an acorn every once in awhile;"
So the old saying goes; and most who hear it have to smile.
We never owned a blind hog so I don't know what one might do,
But if I were a blind hog I'd certainly hope the saying's true.

A blind hog couldn't see where his friends found their meal,
But I guess he might occasionally find one by smell or feel.
Persistence would be needed by our visually challenge friend,
Because persistence often pays off for hard workers in the end.

Persistence requires that we don't give up or quit,
And even when the odds are long we don't stop and sit.
Persistent people are often motivated by a higher goal,
And sometimes many prayers are offered for a lost soul.

Don't give up when the goal is worthy of your effort today,
And don't get sidetracked by what the critics have to say.
Just keep going with your eyes fixed on the final prize,
Because to give up, or to keep going, only you can decide.

The Cherry Tree Adventure

I was about twelve years old and excited to be in the woods.
My Uncle George wanted to flush a turkey for me, if he could.
He provided me with careful instruction as to where I should sit,
And then all I had to do was locate a cherry tree and rest a bit.

My uncle described a destination, a direction and a landmark,
And soon, on my expidition, this novice, happily embarked.
My destination required about two hundred yards of travel,
And for direction, I was to follow an old road with no gravel.

I'd been directed to look for an old cherry tree on the right,
And when I found it I was to wait for a turkey to take flight.
Things went well, I thought; the distance was covered quickly,
However, when I couldn't find the cherry tree, I felt sickly.

My uncle eventually did locate me under a large pine.
He was worried about me, but when I saw him I felt fine.
I didn't see any turkeys and had missed the cherry landmark.
Apparently it died twenty years before and had lost its bark.

The cherry tree was my landmark, but I missed my reservation,
And since my trip was unfamiliar I didn't reach my destination.
I plan to take a much longer trip someday to a place called glory,
And I know, unlike the hunting trip, it'll be a successful story.

The final trip I'm taking is to a place I haven't seen either,
I was once lost, but now I'm found, and in Jesus a believer.
You may never look hopelessly for any old dead cherry trees,
But if you plan to go to heaven, Jesus Christ holds the keys.

The Coat And Tie Rule

I was preaching to our congregation for the very first time.
In fact, preaching had never been an experience of mine.
My preparation, I thought, had been quite extensive,
And I certainly didn't want to say anything offensive.

When the sermon was over and the last hymn was sung,
I waited at the back door to say goodbye to everyone.
Things went well, I thought, until an older man passed by.
He noted, indignantly, that I hadn't worn a coat with my tie.

I like to follow all the rules; I'm a stickler for that,
And when I enter a building, I always remove my hat.
The coat and tie rule; I hadn't seen or heard of that yet
But apparently his expectations for me weren't met.

Later, I took time to researched the preaching attire rule,
Because I hadn't heard about it in church or Sunday school.
When my Bible search finally drew to an unsuccessful end,
I found no verse stating how my coat-less attire might offend.

I came to the conclusion after my research was done,
That the decision of what to wear, was a personal one.
We should give our best to the Master all the time,
But one can wear a coat and tie and never give a dime.

Perhaps, if our desire is to bring glory to the Lord on high,
We should focus on bringing people to Him and put criticism aside.
I'm not sure what attire will be worn as we enter the pearly gates,
But I'm sure none will be standing there in a coat and tie debate.

The Comeback Story

- John 14:3 -

Some teams experience much success on the court or field,
And if you get excited for group of players, you know how I feel.
Excitement can be provided in a number of unforgettable ways,
And I have my fair share of old stories from my playing days.

Often we hear accounts of a winning streak extended,
But we know even if favored any team can be upended.
Fans often become emotionally involved with team success,
But ultimately, we should be satisfied when players do their best.

I had the privilege of competing in many athletic games,
And, even today, I tell the stories and remember player's names.
To be honest, many times, our teams came up a little short,
But that's not the comeback story on which I want to report.

When a team falls behind and winning prospects seem bleak,
Many still dream of a comeback and victory they still seek.
But, alas, even with hopeful hearts and all efforts extended,
Often the comeback doesn't happen before the game has ended.

But there is a wonderful comeback story foretold long ago,
And it will happen for sure; the Bible records clearly show.
Jesus promised to come back someday for all of His own,
And when He does, He'll take us to our forever home.

His comeback wasn't predicted for just a few worthy men,
In fact, it was promised for all who place their trust in Him.
Any player in the game of life, regardless of the scouting report,
Should trust Christ alone; His comeback will not fall short.

The Devil Made Me Do It

It's funny how a classic statement survives the test of time.
What is it about a phrase that makes it a time tested line?
Most remember, many years ago, laughing at my title phrase,
And it's amazing how many people still use it these days.

According to the Bible, the devil does indeed still exist,
And that's important because he can present a harmful risk.
Perhaps a better understanding of the devil's power is needed,
To see if the implied danger warning should be heeded.

Some suggest, the best way to avoid a problem of this kind,
Is to see how much power the devil may have in our time.
The devil does have influence; his activity is far reaching,
But God has much more power according to Bible teaching.

The devil can't make me do things; I have God's power to resist,
And for every Christians this point should never be missed.
We can yield to the devil, and let him have his way,
But God gives us protection to experience victory every day.

The devil does have power but God has so much more,
And since the Bible teaches this, we can know for sure.
Jesus proved His power; when to temptation He never fell,
And since He protects us, we need not submit to Satan's spell.

The Final Chapter

Every book that has chapters has one near the back cover,
And the final chapter may give insight or reveal a twist to discover.
Many authors like to build suspense as the book's pages are turned.
Some may tell of lessons the writer in their lives have learned.

A person's life is much like the book's chapters, in many ways,
Because events happen, like chapters, throughout all our days.
Some people are blessed with longevity and many chapters of life,
But often life is short and chapters may mention a husband or a wife.

Life can be much like a mystery novel in many ways,
Because we don't even know the number of our days.
A comic book, will many times, to us bring a laugh or smile,
And life can take funny turns which brings laughter for a while.

The last chapter is intriguing, just because of when it's written;
Rich or poor, sad or lonely, happiness or perhaps grief stricken.
What will it bring our way when we around that final bend?
There are many unknowns lurking as life nears its earthly end.

Ashes to ashes; dust to dust; we all will from this life pass away,
But if we read the Bible it has much more about life to say.
The final chapter comes only after our earthly life has ended,
And the final chapter is for a Christian by far the most splendid.

Aches and pains acquired; perhaps in chapter three or four,
Won't bother us in heaven which will last forevermore.
So don't be downhearted brother, when life comes to an end.
Faith in Jesus takes us to the final chapter; on Him we can depend.

The Holy Huddle

When our coach said, "huddle up," we all knew what to do.
He wanted us together so his message could get through.
Sometimes he called us in to discuss the details of a play,
And often he announced our practice was over for the day.

Some group planning is important; I think all would agree,
Since without it, my new ideas could only come from me.
I've had a few good ideas, I think, from time to time,
But often, the more successful plans weren't any of mine.

You could think of a committee as a huddle of sorts,
And that's a good place for the sharing of group reports.
Consensus can be reached and they may set noble goals,
But if they stay in the huddle the plan will never unfold.

I recently heard about a holy huddle, organized by a few,
But after years of discussion, progress was long overdue.
The little church with few members wanted to expand,
But none left their holy group huddle to execute the plan.

The people were devout and seldom did anything wrong,
But sadly, they stayed in their holy huddle far too long.
Some of them got too old to work while others passed away,
But none left the holy huddle and only continued to delay.

Christians should gather together and work with one accord.
God tells us to do that, and His instructions can't be ignored.
Unfortunately, even a holy huddle can't accomplish very much,
If we don't reach out to those who need the Master's touch.

The Listener

My Granddaddy was quite old when I arrived on the scene.
He couldn't walk very well, but his hearing was keen.
Granddaddy lived on the first floor of our old country home,
And I visited him often on my way out, when allowed to roam.

He sat in the same old antique chair each and every day,
And was always happy to see me when I returned from play.
I sat close beside granddaddy and told him all that I had done,
He listened quietly to my stores as I recounted each and every one.

There was an old radio which sat on a small table beside his chair,
But he never wanted to listen to it as long as I was there.
He always seemed excited to hear what his grandson had on his mind,
But the thing I remember most about him is that he was always kind.

Granddaddy was never in a hurry like most adults can be,
And he always seemed interested when I sat beside his knee.
One Saturday morning, to my surprise, he wasn't in his chair.
The one who had listened patiently to me, was no longer there.

As I now reflect on this listener and how he cared for me,
I know for sure that he was the kind of person that I want to be.
There are many who struggle today and some may live in fear,
Please Lord, give me enough compassion to lend a listening ear.

The Long Faced Christian

He said he was a Christian. But could that be so?
We couldn't see his heart but on his face it didn't show.

Day after day he lived his life wearing the same frown,
But he spoke of Jesus often to the people in our town.

He said he had burdens that Jesus had taken away,
So why was his face so long each and every day?

He said he was thankful for God's love in his heart,
But it was strange how his face never looked the part.

A smile would seem more appropriate for a man in his position,
But the frown he wore indicated a far more painful condition.

So in conclusion, if you're a Christian, make sure you tell your face,
Because of what Jesus did, you can smile through God's grace.

1 Peter 3;15
But sanctify the Lord God in your hearts: and be ready always to give an answer to every man that asks you a reason of the hope that is in you with meekness and fear.

The Morning Announcements

The announcements must be made every Sunday morning rain or shine,
But this morning that responsibility just happens to be mine.
There's one small problem I noticed this morning which I incurred,
I seem to have misplaced the list of activities this week to be observed.

I'll just have to trust memory today since I've lost my list,
And I certainly hope something important won't be missed.
It shouldn't be hard to come up with this week's activity plan,
But I'd hate to miss something that could help my fellow man.

Oh well; here goes; this will have to be off the cuff,
But I sure don't want to leave out any important stuff.
"God's in charge," that's number one, I know that for sure.
No more important concept than that can long endure.

"God never makes mistakes," that's number two, can't leave that out;
Our Bibles declare this truth often, so there can be little doubt.
As for announcement number three, that's the easiest one.
"Our sin debt can only be forgiven by Jesus," God's only begotten Son.

I can't think of anything more important today than these three,
Because if we believe on Jesus we'll be eternally set free.
We post announcements up front if you need to take a peek,
And they should even work well to be announced again next week.

Oh No: I need to add one more announcement to my posted list,
Because it's so important and I hope no one will ever forget.
"Jesus is coming back," although we don't know the exact day,
But when He does, God's glory will be on full display.

The Old Anvil

There it was, sadly, just resting on the old shop floor,
With some other, now unused items behind the door.
However, the old anvil seemed to draw my interest near,
And I wondered why such a useful thing collected dust here.

Upon further careful inspection I was suddenly amazed,
And saw more value in the anvil upon which I now gazed.
I noticed it was quite rough with hammer marks on it's face,
And I'd never seen one like it around here, or in any place.

The anvil was heavy and weighed well over a hundred pounds,
And it seemed to have a little different shape than any I'd found.
When we picked it up from the floor and placed it on a table,
We saw some letters and numbers stamped, like a kind of label.

The numbers and letters were very hard for us to see,
But they included the name William, and the year 1833.
Someone had hand forged this anvil from a block of steel.
No matter the name of the craftsman a connection to him I feel.

The anvil was used in a formally all black student's school,
And, no doubt, was donated to them as a useful tool.
This item had been hammered years before slavery ended,
And on this old anvil it's maker's livelihood had depended.

We think, perhaps, this old anvil was hand forged by a slave.
Certainly it was donated long after it's maker went to his grave.
We know for sure that the maker worked hard and was useful,
And although it's been 190 years his message is still truthful.

The old anvil was a valuable tool in the workman's hand,
And what he produced with the use of it, was in high demand.
We have tools today and can use them to help people in these parts.
With more loving kindness we may even heal some broken hearts.

The Old Blue Jacket

It's just an old blue jacket, worn so many years ago.
It does have some wear and a few bare threads now show.
The value of the jacket may to many seem quite small,
But to most who wore one, that's not the case at all.

Styles in jackets may have changed often over time,
But all who represent the FFA wear one just like mine.
National blue remains the color with stitches of corn gold,
But the stories of its many wearers continue to unfold.

Some may become farmers and work with plants and soil,
While others may become doctors and in a hospital toil.
The blue jacket won't determine your choice of career,
But it does remain a symbol of values we hold dear.

Yes, it's just an old blue jacket hanging in the closet now,
But the lives of many who wore one were changed somehow.
Respect for others and fair play toward my fellowman,
Are an important part of the old blue jacket's lesson plan.

Dedicated with love and great respect to my friend,
fellow FFA team coach and brother in blue.

Henry Paris
1947 - 2023

The Old Grapevine

- John 15 -

Anticipation and excitement were the words of the day,
Because my search had begun; it was around the first of May.
Spring had brought much new growth in the quiet woods,
As I searched for the place where Great Grandpa's cabin once stood.

The old cabin had been destroyed by fire, but none were hurt.
All that was left were a few large stones protruding from the earth.
The stones were the foundation where his cabin stood long ago,
And I felt a strong connection to them as I searched to and fro.

Just then, I saw what appeared to be, an old grape vine in a tree.
I was amazed to see it; and its sheer size was surprising to me.
The vine, large and twisted, had survived unseen for 100 years,
And the sight of Great Grandpa's grapevine brought me to tears.

The long forgotten vine now only had branches at the very top,
And if you needed grapes, that would be a tough place to shop.
A soft wind surrounded me as I looked up to the rich blue sky.
I lingered at the old cabin site, but only partially understood why.

In the Bible the scriptures make reference to Jesus as the vine.
Believers are called branches; God's order withstands the test of time.
Like the branches on the vine, without Jesus we'd be hopelessly lost.
As we live and grow, remember we were purchased at great cost.

The Old Man Said
John's Story

The old man stood before us; not his normal or preferred place,
But he had an important message and it showed on his face.
He had lived a long life and seen many things in his day,
So we listened closely to what the old man had to say.

He spoke softly but clearly as he told his life's story true,
Of how he had lived his life with some advice for me and you.
The old man left his family early because he disliked rules,
In fact he turned his back on God and even Sunday School.

Surely he knew enough by now to find his own way,
So he found a job far from home without delay.
He quickly found new friends, who were not his friends at all,
And got involved with many things that only bring downfall.

The years for the old man passed and many mistakes were made,
But peace was never found by him in the life he then displayed.
Then a man came to him one day with some advice much needed.
The man spoke of a Savior's love and a message to be headed.

God then worked a miracle in the old man's sinful life,
In fact, it was instantly noticed by the old man's faithful wife.
The sinful things in his life passed away and lost all their charm,
As he drew closer to Jesus and fell into the Saviors loving arms.

The old man had gone astray and had wasted many years,
But God had rescued him and gently removed his tears.
The old man's final plea to each who heard his life's story,
Was for all to come to Jesus and behold His eternal Glory.

The Old Walking Cane

Many have problems which are frankly beyond their control,
And quite often the condition may worsen as we grow old.
Some have a yearning to purchase unneeded things at a store.
We may never use the item; but who can know that for sure?

I made one such purchase quite a few years ago,
And I hope to never need it, but how can I know?
I was shopping at a flea market, and to my surprise,
There was an old walking cane right before my eyes.

The handle was made from antler but the shaft was of oak wood,
And if I had the money, and could buy it, I thought I should.
The lacquer finish on the shaft could be dated, and was very old,
And if I acted quickly enough, to me the old cane would be sold.

The negotiations, as to the price, went for me, very well.
I've seen other old canes bring good money when they sell.
The antler handle had the owner's initials carved at its base,
They were J D M; I wondered what challenges he'd faced.

My hope is that I never need this sturdy old walking aid,
But I think it's worth far more than the small price I paid.
If nothing else, it will serve as a reminder that I am blessed,
Particularly, if I never need to use the cane I now possess.

But, if perchance I need it, or even a more steady support,
I want to go on record as a blessed man in my final report.
God has been my guide and directed my way thus far.
As Christians, please don't forget, just how blessed we are.

The Open Bible

There it was, left open, in full view for all to see;
A Bible placed on a small table to be read, no fee.
Many passed by without a glance upon its pages,
Simply ignoring the wisdom found therein for all ages.

Day after day many rush by fixed on some other mission,
And never notice this Bible left in the open position.
Just a glance, that wouldn't hurt, perhaps a verse or phrase,
We might find those words helpful in so many ways.

Anyone can turn its pages, a Bible should be read,
But sadly, some use a Bible for decoration instead.
Some may think it helpful to use a Bible in this way,
But a Bible should be read and in our lives displayed.

1 Thessalonians 4:13-14

But I would not have you ignorant, brethren, concerning them which are asleep, that ye sorrow not, even as others which have no hope. For if we believe that Jesus died and rose again, even so them which sleep in Jesus, will God bring with him.

The Pickup Game

I've played a lot of basketball; you can shoot most anywhere.
My friends and I played often; rain or shine, we were there.
Pickup games were exciting against people you didn't know,
Because we all had a few moves we sometimes liked to show.

When a new player arrived on the pickup basketball scene,
We just picked the new kid up on one of the regular teams.
The rosters were never set; they changed from day to day;
We never worried about those details; we just liked to play.

So many memories were made, and we enjoyed every game,
But old people can't do that now; too many aches and pains.
I've been thinking; are pickup games actually out of the picture?
In fact; I think the concept may be implied in the Holy Scriptures.

Some of us can't bend over these days like we did in the past,
But if you are inclined to give up; hold on a minute; not so fast.
Do you, perhaps, have a friend who can't get out of bed anymore?
Just pick up your phone and call him; he'd be encouraged for sure.

How about your sick friend who might enjoy a thoughtful tweet?
How about a lonely person, you can text and never leave your seat?
You could even pick up a pen and pad and send a kind letter today,
And that might bless someone who does things the oldfashoned way.

When I pick up the newspaper and read of people in need,
I wonder why I've waited so long to plant more loving seeds.
Sadly, It's not a game anymore; real life is hard for many it seems,
Pick up what you have and spread God's love, if you're on His team.

The Poor Rich Man

- Luke 16 -

We don't have a lot of information on how he lived his life,
And we don't even know if the poor rich man had a wife.
The things we do know are recorded in God's word,
And his may be the saddest story some have ever heard.

We're told he lived a blessed life and wore purple with linen fine,
Apparently, in his life he had everything, and at a full table dined.
I'm glad this account is recorded in the Bible for me and you,
Because the rest of his story is a warning for us; sad but true.

There was another man mentioned in this rich man's woeful lesson,
His name was Lazarus, but his life's story mentioned no possessions.
In fact, Lazarus was a beggar who waited for the rich man's crumbs,
And he laid near the city gate, perhaps with the deaf and dumb.

Lazarus had many open wounds and suffered daily great dismay,
And we're told the city stray dogs licked his wounds every day.
We're also told when Lazarus died an angel took him to glory.
However, when the poor rich man died, his was a different story.

Lazarus went to heaven and rested on father Abraham's chest,
But the fate received by the rich man didn't match his life's success.
We read of a large expanse between Lazarus and the rich man,
And sadly, after death none can ever cross this eternal span.

This account was told by Jesus and recorded in God's word,
And gives a glimpse of our fate if salvation's message goes unheard.
Heaven does exist my friend, and sadly, likewise so does hell,
And only by faith in Jesus can we in heaven someday dwell.

The Rich Man

Rich men seem to be a topic of some people in our day,
And many listen to these men to hear what they may say.
Perhaps some may listen to find the secret of their success,
While others just keep toiling on and daily do their best.

What is it about people that makes them rich or poor,
And what standards must be met to know richness for sure?
We know money and land can be measured for an indication,
But these things are affected by depressions and inflation.

I once knew a man who said he was a very wealthy man,
But I didn't observe these riches with a casual scan.
He said his riches could not be observed with the naked eye,
And most of his riches were reserved for the sweet by and by.

He said God had surely blessed him with riches untold,
But these riches could not be, by man, bought or sold.
The endowment he had received was part of a gifted prize.
It came to him freely but its value could not be denied.

Peace and joy he had received, with full pardon for his soul,
The price of these things was paid in full on Calvary's knoll.
He said all men and women could be rich in this eternal way,
One must only believe on Jesus and walk with Him each day.

The Scary Old Man

Rumors were swirling; I don't know exactly when they began,
But one of the kids at church thought he'd seen a scary old man.
We all had concerns, because this could be a very serious thing,
And we all hoped to avoid the situation that could bring.

We each kept our eyes open for the guy, particularly at night,
But we all know bad things can happen even in broad daylight.
The police were quickly alerted and increased their patrol,
But for many of our members, frankly, worry took a heavy toll.

Someone noticed an old picture hanging on our church back wall,
And the former pastor depicted apparently never smiled at all.
Could one of our children have noticed this former preacher,
And been frightened by this old brother's stern and stoic features?

When I got up early this morning and in the mirror gazed,
I hardly recognized the scary old man, and I stood amazed.
My posture was good but my happy smile looked like a frown.
Could it be that the kids thought I was the scary old man in town?

As I quietly stared at the grumpy figure, also staring back at me,
I was convicted, because it's the person that our church kids see.
I'm happy that I have Jesus and eternal life in my heart,
But sadly, my face didn't get the message, or look the part.

Scary old men do exist; we all know that to be true,
But Christians should never look scary when the day is through.
Since peace, joy and hope all reside in every Christian's heart,
Let's make sure we tell our faces, so they can look the part.

The Silk Purse And The Sow's Ear

"You can't make a silk purse out of a sow's ear," so we're told.
Many old sayings like this have circulated since the days of old.
What is it about the silk purse that affords it worldly acclaim,
And what causes the sow's ear to be less recognized for fame?

God made the old sow, and He created her ancestors too,
So He must have made her prophetic ears, since that's true.
Now we all know each silk thread was made by a tiny worm,
Does the sow's ear look so bad, with silk's source now learned?

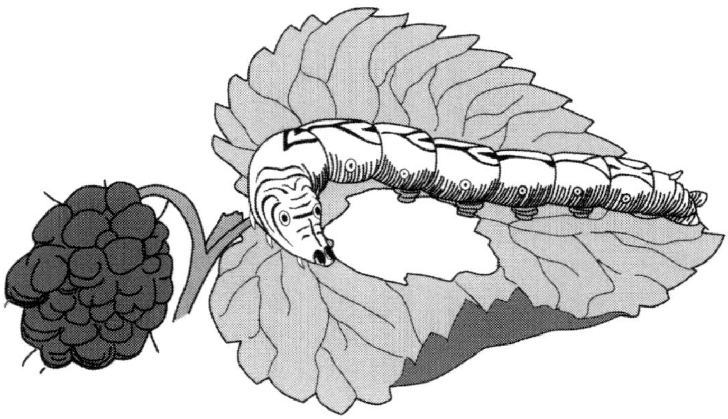

The Undercover Christian

I never knew a detective who had gone undercover,
Or perhaps, if I did, his mission was never discovered.
Undercover detectives must be secretive and discrete,
And to do that, they act like the normal people we meet.

I've met some people who have some things to hide,
And although I was a curious; I worked hard not to pry.
The most unusual case I think I ever actually observed,
Was a man who was reluctant to reveal the master he served.

The man was a Christian and attended a church down the street,
And he was quite outgoing and a nicer man you wouldn't meet.
When he had an opportunity to speak a word about the Lord,
He was reluctant to say anything about the one he said he adored.

He quite freely told people the name of the church he attended,
But was reluctant to mention the Lord on which he depended.
He said he was thankful for all the things he possessed,
But he never mentioned the name of the Savior he professed.

He did occasionally invite a friend to church to enjoy a dinner,
But he never mentioned how Jesus had come to save a sinner.
He liked his pastor and attended church most every Sunday,
But sadly, he seemed to forget what he'd heard by Monday.

Unfortunately, undercover Christians do exist, I must confess,
But isn't it better, when about our Lord and Savior we profess?
Some haven't heard the message of Jesus and His saving grace,
So if you're a Christian tell others and don't just take up space.

They Never Met

I heard about an interesting lady who'd traveled far and wide.
She spoke often of her exploits which couldn't be denied.
She had met movie stars and some world leaders too.
She packed much into her life before living was through.

She studied many religions as she traveled all over the world,
But she was raised in a Christian home when she was a girl.
She had attended Sunday School; and even loved her teachers,
And also attended morning services and heard many preachers.

Her varied experiences had led her to have mixed emotions,
Because she had entertained many religious notions.
She professed to be a good person, which none denied,
And many kind things were said about her when she died.

This lady's story, like ours, doesn't end at the grave.
There's another chapter according to instruction Jesus gave.
God said it's not by righteous works which we have done.
Salvation is only bestowed on those who meet God's Son.

Jesus came to earth to seek and save those which were lost,
And He paid for their sins; His perfect life was the cost.
To receive salvation one must believe on God's only Son,
And for all who do that, eternal life is gloriously won.

The dear lady who'd traveled to many places far and wide,
Had sadly not accepted Jesus as her Lord before she died.
Her chance was like ours; to meet Jesus before her life's end.
It's our most important choice; on Jesus only we must depend.

Those Teenagers

One morning our adult Sunday School class was about to start,
But one of our members had something troubling on her heart.
She was now in her eighties, but said she'd been faithful in her day,
However, this morning she wanted to vent, by what she had to say.

For years she'd served; and said her commitment never wavered.
When telling of her works, the story was by her even savored.
Lately she had made a profound and alarming observation.
Teenagers, she was sure, would bring the downfall of our nation.

Teenagers were unruly; about them she had nothing good to say,
And if something didn't happen soon they may lead the world astray.
Having now heard her discourse, I felt compelled to reply.
I loved teenagers and was glad to tell this angry lady why.

I had been a teacher and had known teens for over a generation,
And felt they could be taught to be the leaders of our nation.
I asked the lady a question and wondered how she would reply.
Could she give me the names of three teenagers who lived nearby?

She thought for a moment, then confessed that she knew no names,
But she was convinced they had evil intentions just the same.
Then I gave some timely good advice, as she listened to my words.
Go tell those teenagers about Jesus; they may not have ever heard.

1 Timothy 4:12
Let no man despise thy youth; but be thou an example of the believers, in word, in conversation, in charity, in spirit, in faith, in purity.

Three Bears

I heard some commotion just over a small hill in the woods,
And I thought I might investigate the source, if I could.
Getting close should be easy; but I mustn't move too quick,
Because in the summertime the foliage often can be thick.

I was shocked when I spotted the source of the noise,
And frankly, it was very difficult to maintain my poise.
There they were; a mere fifty feet in front of me,
And I must admit, they were a beautiful sight to see.

There were three of them; so I must watch my step.
Frankly, what I was now watching, was hard to accept.
The first one was more aggressive; with teeth now displayed,
Number two quietly rested, while the others passed the day.

Most would be fearful to be so close to three wild bears,
And I'd never experienced a situation like this anywhere.
I was fairly sure I hadn't been detected as of yet,
But when they do noticed me, I may have some regret.

Just then I woke up, from what must have been a dream,
And if you're a dreamer you probably know what I mean.
When I calmed down and my heart rate slowed a bit,
I turned the light on and felt much better with it lit.

I had dreamed of three small bear cubs frolicking at play,
No need to worry; dream bears can't hurt us anyway.
People are sometimes fearful, and often prone to worry,
But things we imagine can't hurt us even it they're furry.

Too Many Cooks

Mama was a great cook; the very best I ever knew,
And she seemed to enjoy cooking for our little crew.
Mashed potatoes with homemade milk gravy on the side;
You couldn't beat that no matter how hard you tried.

She also made spoon bread; out of the oven piping hot,
And you could eat a bowl of that; hungry or not.
Chicken and dumplings with fresh biscuits piled high,
They didn't last very long, so you best not be shy.

I don't know how she did it, but I enjoyed every meal,
And if you had a Mom like mine you know how I feel.
Our kitchen wasn't large but Mom enjoyed it just fine,
And even if I was busy I made it to meals on time.

There were only two kitchen rules for us to obey;
Mom was in charge of the kitchen and had the final say.
If she needed help she was more than willing to ask,
But she made it clear, in our house, cooking was her task.

Her actions demonstrated that no suggestions were needed,
And since she was in charge, her rules were to be heeded.
It's funny how sometimes we think our way is best,
And then often, to have our way, becomes our final quest.

Kitchen rules are needed; too many cooks do spoil the pot,
And if we all demand to have our way, that happens a lot.
Jesus came to accomplish a task that only He could do.
His way is best for everyone; and even for good cooks too.

What We Can't Do

What we can't do, may well change as the years go by,
And if you've been around for a while you should know why.
If we long for usefulness with a particular important task,
What we can do, may be the better question to be asked.

As children, what we couldn't do was dictated by others,
And quite often the mandates were enforced by our mothers.
As we got a little older and school became part of our day,
It was our teachers who regulated our behavioral display.

Most of us have now arrived at our post schoolyard time,
And the choice of what I do, or don't do, is mostly mine.
There's little use in attempting what I can't do anymore,
But what I can do, should be my focus even more.

Focus is important if what I can do is to be achieved,
And often what I should do is dictated by what I believe.
If I think my responsibility is to help my fellowman,
Then I should help my earthly brothers in any way I can.

If we believe we're called to serve a Holy God above,
Then we should reach out to those in need because of God's love.
What we can't do doesn't matter as much as we thought before.
Just practice what we should do; people in need can't be ignored.

Word Problems

Problems are a fact of life and affect everyone we know;
They've always plagued mankind, the written records show.
Problems are often classified into many different categories,
And they can even have an impact on someone's life story.

In math class we were all given problems to be solved,
And to accomplish that task it often took much resolve.
Whether addition, subtraction, multiplication or division,
Some thought was required to bring each one to submission.

Many seemed to struggle with word problems, most of all,
Because they used both words and numbers, as I now recall.
If Sally owned three dogs, one duck and three small kittens,
On the total line at the bottom, a seven should be written.

Even as adults, we often still have problems with words,
And the choices we make can cause harm to be incurred.
Unkind or thoughtless words are far too often spoken,
And the words we select can cause a heart to be broken.

Once a word is spoken, like in math, there is a result,
Whether on the school yard or in a gathering among adults.
If we choose words carefully and more compassion show,
We can often help resolve problems wherever we may go.

Worry

I know I shouldn't worry, but it's often what I do,
It never seems to help but somehow I make it through.
I worry most often when something is out of my control,
But I must admit that worry is beginning to take a toll.

Trusting is a better option when a situation needs to change,
But worry comes much more easily; isn't that strange?
For those who have trusted Jesus to take them by the hand,
Surely asking for His help today would be a better plan.

He promised never to leave me; forsaking me He won't do,
So why have I worried so often when the day is through?
Worry reveals a weakness in those who often take part,
Because trusting Jesus always happens in our hearts.

Our minds are wonderful and we use them every day,
But God never intended minds to take our fears away.
Trust and faith will give us complete victory for sure,
But worry can only give us endless pain to endure.

Philippians 4; 6-7

Be careful for nothing; but in everything by prayer and supplication with thanksgiving let your requests be made known unto God. And the peace of God which passes all understanding shall keep your hearts and minds through Christ Jesus.